Passive Income

Learn How to Make Money Online and Become Financially Free

James Cheney

James Cheney

Table of Contents

∗ ∗ ∗

Introduction	v
Chapter 1: Pros and Cons of Passive Income	1
Chapter 2 : Passive Income 1: Writing E-Books	7
Benefits of Writing an E-book	8
Writing the E-book	10
Publishing an E-book	13
Marketing Your E-book	14
Chapter 3: Passive Income 2: Amazon FBA	15
What Is FBA?	16
Benefits of FBA	17
How to Get into the FBA Program	19
How FBA Helps You Earn Passive Income	21
Chapter 4: Passive Income 3: Email Marketing	23
What Is E-mail Marketing?	23
Benefits of E-mail Marketing	24

Two Things You Need for E-mail Marketing	26
Creating Newsletters	28
How to Earn with E-mail Marketing	29
Important Tips	30
Chapter 5: Passive Income 4: Affiliate Marketing	33
What Is Affiliate Marketing?	34
Benefits of Affiliate Marketing	35
How to Become an Affiliate Marketer	37
Independent Websites	39
Affiliate Marketplaces	40
Joint Venture or Partnership	41
More Tips in Affiliate Marketing	42
Chapter 6 : Passive Income 5: Create an Online Course	45
What Is an Online Course?	45
Benefits of Creating an Online Course	47
How to Design an Online Course	48
How to Market Online Courses	52
Pricing	53
Chapter 7: Passive Income 6: Create Viral Videos	55
What Is a Viral Video?	56
How Do You Make Money in a Viral Video?	57
How to Make Your Video Viral	58

Production	59
Shooting and Editing	60
Publishing	61
Chapter 8: Passive Income 7: Trading Domain Names	63
Understanding Domain Names	64
The Power of Trading Domain Names	65
How to Trade a Domain Name	66
Important Tips in Trading Domain Names	69
Conclusion	70

Passive Income

Introduction

* * *

A proverb says: "Give a man a fish and he eats for a day. Teach him how to fish and you feed him for a lifetime."

While growing up, I had the penchant to teach people. I remember when my friends struggled with mathematics, they would be all around our living room on weekends as I pretended to be our teacher. It was not the best imitation, but I believed I was good in what I did since we succeeded in getting high grades in the subject.

When I was in college, I thought about teaching, but other interests won me over. However, that did not stop me from sharing whatever knowledge I had to whoever was willing to listen.

At this point, I want to do just that—the only difference is that I am using a different medium, which is the Internet. Interestingly, this is also the tool we are going to take advantage of exhaustively in order to earn not just any other income but passive income.

Passive income, you say? Yes, passive income.

There are many different types of income. If you have a home and you are leasing it, then you earn a rental income. If you are doing business, the money you earn is called revenue. If you have savings in your bank account, more likely, it is earning interest income.

But even if you have these different kinds of income, they are still classified into two: active and passive.

As its name suggests, **active income** is the earnings you get for the services performed or rendered. These include your wages or salaries, bonuses, incentives, commissions, and tips. In other words, unless you do something, you do not earn anything.

Passive income, on the other hand, is the earnings you get with less effort than what you do in an active income. One of its most distinctive features is automation. Once you set your earning model up, you can earn money even if you are hardly doing anything!

A very good example is a rental property.

This e-book, however, will not talk about leasing your real estate. Rather, I intend to teach you how to earn passive income using the Internet. In the next chapter, I will outline the different reasons why.

Right now, my only request is that you pay attention as I impart the lessons I gained through many years of trial and error, failures, and eventually successes.

Chapter 1: Pros and Cons of Passive Income

* * *

Before we get into the nitty gritty of the theme of the e-book, let us talk about the advantages and the disadvantages of trying to earn a passive income online. This is very important for two reasons:

- **I want you to make smart decisions.** I once had a friend who decided to do affiliate marketing simply because "Well, everybody is doing it!" It did not take long before he drained his bank account with no positive outcome of his efforts. Plenty of factors came into play, but one of the main reasons was he did not think things through.

- **We have to set the right expectations.** Please do not believe everything you hear and read online. These include that earning money online is easy-peasy. No, it is not. The only thing that is easy is a get-rich-quick scheme, and we all know that it almost always does not end well.

Why Do Passive Income

Let us begin with the positives. Why does it make sense to perform passive income?

1. You can earn money without really working.

Ask anybody these days, and you will know that the most precious commodity today is time. Everyone is busy, and whether we like it or not, we feel as if 24 hours a day is never enough for the things that we do. This explains why we are incredibly fond of "instant" products.

Besides, working is stressful, regardless of how much you love your job. There will be a lot of days when you have to drag yourself out of bed to get to work. Doesn't everyone look forward to Fridays and weekends? We just love Saturday mornings when we can sleep in.

The beauty of passive income is you can earn even if you are doing well, basically, nothing.

However, once the book is up, it has the opportunity to earn money now. You do not have to constantly update it or write some more chapters. It is basically there in Amazon to earn you money.

2. There is no limit to the income you can earn.

While I love the first reason, this is my favorite. One of the biggest disadvantages of active income is its income potential is limited. Sure, you can be earning hundreds of thousands of dollars a year, but then, you cannot get more out of the salary and incentives stated in your contract. If it says you are earning $30,000 a month, then that is what you are going to get regardless of how much effort, hard work, and overtime you clock in.

Passive income, meanwhile, does not have restriction. As I would like to say, the sky is the limit. Going back to our e-book example previously, let us further assume that 3 people, on the average, buy your book on a daily basis.

Now let us do some math: 3 people per day x 30 days a month x $20 each e-book

This gives you $1,800 for the e-book! And how many times do you update the book in a month again? Nada. You can safely say that $1,800 is the amount you earn from doing almost nothing.

Simply put, with passive income, you can earn not only through automation but also through replication.

3. Anybody can do it!

Usually, when you want to earn active income, you need to possess a certain skill set and even educational background. With passive income, it is everybody's ball game.

Of course, you also need to have certain skills, but the great thing is earning does not require you certifications and degrees. Furthermore, with so many ways to earn passive income, you can certainly find one that you believe that you can do or at least try with highest confidence.

4. It offers you more freedom.

Whenever I think about this, I am always reminded of Tim Ferriss, the author of the NY Times best-selling book called *4-Hour Workweek*. If you are wondering why it is titled as such, it is because he works for around that duration every week. How much time do you spend in your present work? Most probably, you have a 9-5 job, which means you work for at least 40 hours each week.

Like Ferriss, I have learned to take mini vacations than a grand vacation whenever I could afford a leave, worse when I am already retired (if I have not kicked the bucket yet). This simply means I get to pursue the things I want to do at my own pace while still earning.

Why You Should Not

No earnings model can be considered perfect. The same thing goes with passive income. As I mentioned, one of our objectives for this chapter is to set the right expectations, and to do that, we have to be honest on its cons.

1. It still needs hard work.

If you have not noticed it yet, I never once claim that passive income means earning money with no work at all.

Passive Income

In fact, you will find yourself spending a lot of time in the beginning of the journey.

Consider this passive income endeavor as a business that has baby steps before you can achieve success. Further, like a machine, it needs to be calibrated before it becomes automated. And even if it is already automated, you still have to upgrade it regularly to ensure that it continues to work well.

2. It can still end up as a failure.

Like any other activity in the world, passive income models can end up a success or a failure. There are many reasons why your passive income strategies will fail—and it could range from lack of the right set of skill or poor attitude toward it—but the bottom line is that you still have to hope for the best but prepare for the worst.

3. It requires money.

I can vividly remember a conversation I had with a friend with whom I discussed passive income. He was already convinced to doing it until we reached about costs. He was really surprised when I told him that he might end up spending at least a thousand dollars if he wished to write an e-book.

In whatever you do, you need to invest, and passive income requires money as well.

4. It can be unstable.

While passive income can provide you with plenty and very huge opportunities to earn money, it can also become unstable, which usually happens when the demand for the product you have created goes down. There is no one buying the book, for example. But then again, this is why you should regularly update your product and even your skill, continue to invest, replicate and even diversify.

Indeed, passive income has its own risks and uncertainties, but based on experience, the benefits definitely outweigh the disadvantages. Moreover, I am here to show you the many ways to earn good passive income online while avoiding the common and sometimes costly pitfalls. This way, you are getting the best exchange value for your investment.

Chapter 2 : Passive Income 1: Writing E-Books

* * *

Who does not know Amazon? The Amazon Prime Day is now considered as the biggest holiday for online retailers ever with estimated sales of more than $500 million IN ONE DAY! Can you actually believe that?

In fact, there was a time when Amazon did not do so well, especially during its first few years, yet one of the reasons for its success over the years is books.

Amazon does not just sell e-books, and if you browse through its lists, many of the retailers still carry paperbacks and even hardcovers. But then again, most of them also have e-book equivalents.

What is an e-book? As its name suggests, e-book stands for electronic book. It is mainly the digitalization of the pages that you have grown to love so reading them becomes more convenient.

You can now read them on the Internet or store them in skinny devices like tablets or e-book readers, which can actually store hundreds of books. It is like bringing an entire library with you wherever you go.

The great thing is reading is not the only thing that you can do with e-books. You can make an awesome passive business with it.

Benefits of Writing an E-book

Writing an e-book is not really easy. However, there are dozens of reasons why you should at least consider one:

It is such a nifty project.

One of the things I love about making e-books such as this one is that it gets me to fulfill two objectives: become an author and share information with other people like you. I can contribute to every person's learning process, whether they eventually like the book or not.

You can earn money from it. Oh, there are so many ways to generate money from e-books. Here are two of them:

- **Sell it directly.** Basically, you write and sell your book to different marketplaces, which you will know later on. E-books these days are sold in a wide range of prices. You can even find books that are available for pennies. Usually, however, you can sell it for at least $15.

It may come as cheap, but just think about this: if you sell 100 copies of them (or that is about less than 4 a day), you have $1,000 a month. If you keep on producing books, then, of course, you will earn some more.

- **Be an affiliate marketer.** In chapter 4, I will talk more extensively about affiliate marketing, but just to give you an idea, you can sell other people's products for a commission every time someone buys them through you. In other words, even if you are not the one who wrote the book, you can still earn something from it.

It is an incredibly growing market.

The e-book market is getting more dynamic, with more people choosing to become independent publishers and with websites such as Amazon offering tools to make publishing even more convenient and cheaper.

Creating Topics for E-book

What is the subject of your e-book? Other experts will tell you to go for topics you like or passionate about whether it is homes, sports, pets, etc. While that is a good advice, that is not entirely helpful. Here is why: not all topics sell.

Keep in mind that our goal in writing an e-book is not only to share information but also make money from it, so we should be able to generate sales. What should you do then?

Find a subject that interests you then dig deeper then (1) find the market trends and (2) be as specific as you can.

For instance, say, you are interested in homes. If you look at trends in this category, you will find out that there is an increasing demand and interest in small spaces and tiny houses. Thus, you might focus on these sub-topics.

Then you can further narrow it down. What about small spaces or tiny houses you wish to talk about? You can perhaps create a DIY book or, if you are good at carpentry, a collection of furniture plans that are great for these types of houses.

Writing the E-book

Now that you have a clear idea of the subject, you can then proceed to writing. At this point, you have two choices: you can do it yourself or you can hire a writer.

When should you hire a writer?

Consider getting a writer if:

- o You do not have the time to write.
- o Your writer has a more extensive knowledge about the subject than you do.
- o You do not know how to write.

- You want someone to double-check your work before it gets published.

There are hundreds of e-book writers all around the world today, and finding one should not be difficult.

BUT BE WARNED: Not all writers are great as they seem. Do not be afraid to ask for portfolio or other credentials to prove that they are legitimate and are capable of writing your e-book. If possible, go for writers that already have some reviews or ask for references from them.

Make sure that your writers are reachable and that they are committed to communicate with you. With so many options for messaging, lack of communication should no longer be a problem.

As much as possible, too, work with only one writer. This way, the style and tone of the entire e-book is consistent.

What if you decide to write it yourself?

I personally like to write the e-book myself. It gives me a different sense of fulfillment to create something from scratch. Besides, there are already a lot of tools to help writing more manageable despite my super-crazy schedule.

- **E-book Calendar:** This works similarly as an editorial or blog calendar. What I do is to map out dates when I should complete each chapter or stages of the e-book. If you have a writer, you can also share this calendar so you can track milestones.

- **Mind Map:** One of the biggest challenges you will experience in writing an e-book, or any book for that matter, is a writer's block. This simply means that no matter how much you try, you just do not know what to write. Not only is it frustrating, but it also dampens your momentum and forces you to change your calendar.

  That is why I use a mind map, which is a process of building ideas out of a central theme. You can imagine a tree, which represents your main ideas, branching out and creating leaves, which are then your sub-ideas. These sub-ideas can then generate sub-sub-ideas, so on and so forth.

  Basically, I write a general topic and then create "branches" and place them wherever they seem fit. With the use of a software, I can edit my concepts with great ease, but you can still do this even without one or using the Internet.

  If mind mapping is complex for you, creating an outline will do.

- **Word Processor:** Of course, you need something to write on, in this case, it is a word processor such as Microsoft Word. However, I also know of other people who are using alternatives such as Open

Office. You can also use the online version of Microsoft Word, which is in Google Drive.

- o **E-book Formatter:** E-books are sold in different formats such as epub, although I personally prefer PDF because it is more popular and works in multiple devices as long as they have Adobe Reader.

You might also need cloud services such as Dropbox and Google Drive, especially if you are always on the go. This way, you can write and edit anytime and anywhere.

TAKE NOTE: While many of these programs have free features, they can be limited. To take advantage, you might have to pay premium or subscription.

Publishing an E-book

Now that you have an e-book, the next step is publishing. Today you can find different types of publishers out there including traditional houses. It is important that you take the time to get to know them for the following reasons:

- Royalty (including how much percentage sales goes to author and how soon you receive your royalty)
- Author support
- Book format
- Audience reach

Normally authors go for the likes of Lulu and Amazon Direct Publishing since they are already established. However, you should also know that you do have other choices. These include:

- Payhip, which offers 100 percent royalty, hosting, payment, and fulfillment
- Booktango, which can provide designs for book cover
- BookBaby, which allows you to sell your e-book to different partner retailers including Barnes & Noble and Amazon
- E-Junkie, which sells PDF e-books

Marketing Your E-book

Many publishers will assist you in marketing your e-books, but that does not mean you have to completely rely on their efforts. You also need to do your own starting with the following:

- Create a landing page, which is basically one full page that talks comprehensively about the e-book.
- Go social. Sign up in Facebook, Twitter, and other social media and networking accounts where your audience are more likely to be part of to provide short bursts of updates on the e-book.
- Make a teaser video!
- Look for affiliate marketers.
- Do e-mail marketing (we will discuss about this in greater detail later).

- Build a blog where you can interact with your customers, fans, etc.
- Promote it in Reddit. You will be surprised how active members are.

Are you ready to begin your e-book writing journey?

Chapter 3: Passive Income 2: Amazon FBA

* * *

How often do you shop online? I am not a huge shopper, but I know a lot of friends who do, and they can spend thousands of dollars a year. In fact, e-commerce is crazy these last few years that you can purchase anything you like with a few clicks.

Do you need some bread? Go online.
How about flowers? Go online.
Perhaps you are looking for a car or a home? Yes, you can now go online.

The e-commerce industry is huge. E-retail sales as of 2015 had already breached the $300 billion mark, and we are just talking about the US market alone. .

Jack Ma—the owner of Alibaba, a fast-rising online marketplace primarily for businesses—is now one of the richest men in the world because of this business model.

While there are already hundreds of marketplaces in the Internet, one of the biggest, if not the largest, is Amazon.

Amazon itself has its own products and services. Kindle, for one, is an exclusive Amazon product, which means they build and sell them. But majority of the items you see in the website are sold by thousands of their retailers—and you can be one of them through the website's program called Fulfillment by Amazon (FBA).

What Is FBA?

For you to understand what FBA ends, we have to know first how a complete purchase happens.

In the brick-and-mortar store, when you want to buy something, you walk in, check out the products on the shelves, and if there is something that you like, you pick it up or put it in the basket, head to the cashier, pay the bill, and walk out of the store with the paper bag on hand.

Online, it is slightly different. You go to the website, check out the products on the page, click the item you like, press checkout in the shopping cart page, pay using different options such as credit cards, then wait for the product to be shipped to your doorstep within a few days or weeks depending on where you live.

What you are not familiar with is what happens behind the scene as soon as you submit your order:

- Once the vendors see the order, they look into their inventory.
- If the item is in stock, they pack it using their customized packaging or wrap, along with the return label.
- They then ship it to the best local courier or they have the item picked up from their location.
- Then the courier ships the item.

This entire process is called fulfillment, which is now being offered by Amazon.

You may ask, "Why would Amazon offer it when you, as a seller, can already do it?" Here are some of the best reasons why:

Benefits of FBA

You do not have to worry about inventory.

Let me tell you, storing your items in your house works only if you are selling light and small products. It also works only if you have a very small inventory. For example, if you are selling toys, a few hundreds of them will probably go well in your home. Anything more than that, your place becomes messy. Most of all, it is difficult to manage your inventory.

That can be a problem. What if you have sold a product that turns out to be out of stock? You can ruin your own reputation.

With Amazon's FBA, you can take advantage of:

- Expansive Amazon-manned warehouses, which are located in many different parts of the world,
- Thousands of professional Amazon staff, who does the management of inventory, packing, and shipping for you
- Free pickup from your location, which is cool considering the number of items you are planning on selling

You get the backing of a well-trusted brand.

There is a good reason why Amazon is one of the best and most popular marketplaces in the world today: they do great work. Of course, not everyone is happy about it, but most are.

The good news is if you do FBA, you can use the Amazon's name to your leverage:

- You will have Amazon's support staff, who will handle shipping, returns, and refunds on your business's behalf
- Have your products sold in Amazon Prime. This is a very exclusive and immensely popular service

offered by Amazon to their customers, and many people love it because of fast shipping.

Why is this great for you? If your product becomes part of Amazon Prime, it means your customers gets to enjoy the same privilege.

The faster the shipment is completed, the higher your credibility goes. The more you are credible, the more you gain customers' trust. When customers trust you, they recommend you. By simply offering quick and affordable shipping through FBA, you can boost your business profit.

- Your products get to enjoy a wider reach. When your product becomes part of Amazon Prime, it can also be listed in Canada and Mexico Amazon websites, which means you can now have more customers. Note, though, that Amazon does not limit itself in these regions. For the most competitive shipping fees, your product can go anywhere.

The bottom line is this: **With FBA, the only thing you have to worry about is sales.**

How to Get into the FBA Program

There are two ways on how to participate in the FBA program. If you are already a seller in Amazon, you just have to **add an FBA account.** Otherwise, you have to open a seller account then include an FBA account.

Once you have done that, you can now proceed with the remaining steps:

1. **Upload your products in your page.** At this point, your products should not go live first (or available for purchase) since they still have to be picked up by Amazon. If you already have an inventory of the goods, then you can seamlessly integrate that with Amazon's API to avoid common issues with inventory like redundant products on the list.

2. **Prepare the products for pick-up.** Amazon recommends that the items are already "e-commerce ready," which simply means Amazon will not have problems packing and shipping the goods to your customers. Items, for example, may have to be protected by bubble wraps. If the product is composed of parts, then you must make sure that all of the components are complete and intact.

3. **Ship your products to Amazon.** Amazon has several transport carrier partners that can offer you excellent discounts.

You and the customer will know that it is fulfilled by Amazon when the product page has something like this:

> Price: $57.94 & FREE Shipping. Details
>
> In stock on July 22, 2016.
> Order it now.
> Sold by Mr. Peanut's Premium Products and **Fulfilled by Amazon**.
>
> Size: **Large 27.6" x 20.5" x 20.5"**
>
> | Small 19.5" x 13.5" x 13.5" | Medium 23.6" x 16.5" x 16.5" |
> |---|---|
> | $42.94 | $49.94 |
> | **Large 27.6" x 20.5" x 20.5"** $57.94 | X - Large 32" x 22.8" x 22.8" $66.94 |

And as you can see on the image above, the vendor is able to maximize the inventory management software as it reflects when the item is going to be available. Customers can also know if the item is legible for free shipping.

Costing

Amazon FBA is a premium service, which means that you still have to pay for it to take advantage of all the benefits. So how much will it cost you? It depends on many things, including the products that you sell and where the items were sold.

How FBA Helps You Earn Passive Income

"Passive selling": This simply means that you can still sell even if you are not doing the selling yourself. Sounds confusing? Let me explain.

As mentioned, once the product is shipped to and received by Amazon, you can just focus on marketing. And if you have excellent marketing, then everything becomes autopilot. Customers seek and go to your Amazon page, order the product, and Amazon ships. That's it! Your job at this point is to make sure that you can cover the fees of the service.

Now what if you do not have a product to sell? Source them out in many different places. As mentioned, you can go to Alibaba or Salehoo. You can also sell local products.

Affiliate marketing: I will talk about affiliate marketing more comprehensively in the later chapters, but this passive income technique is great for people who (1) do not have the products to sell, (2) do not want to deal with inventory, and (3) are happy earning commission from every sale.

As an affiliate marketer, you can focus on products that are under the FBA program to promote to your target market. Once the customers are able to experience the benefit of the FBA program, there is a very high chance they will come back to you to buy more products. Moreover, you are not limited to only one retailer or product. You can sell as many items as you like!

Chapter 4: Passive Income 3: Email Marketing

* * *

A long time ago, probably 30 years ago, I can remember my mom receiving these colorful papers she would get from our mailbox. I was very young then, so I did not know any better what they were. However, I can also remember how she would sit on the porch, browse through the pages, and list down things on a paper.

When I was in my early teens, I had a better idea what these "colorful papers" were. They were then called brochures and catalogues. Not only that, as my mother was getting older and her eyesight became poorer, the job of ordering items rested on me.

These types of promotional materials are part of direct marketing. Today some companies still do that, but more people are embracing the evolution of direct marketing called e-mail marketing.

What Is E-mail Marketing?

James Cheney

Statistics say that almost every person in the Internet has at least one e-mail address, which suggests that it is possible there are more e-mail addresses than there are people online.

E-mail stands for electronic mail, and yes, it is the digital version of the regular mail you receive in a PO or mailbox at home. It can be considered as your "residential address" in cyberspace. It is how people are able to communicate with you for whatever reason, whether it is to ask how you are, offer you a job, and even sell products and services, just like in the old days of direct marketing.

While a person can have as many e-mail addresses as they like, each of them will be unique, which makes the system even more special.

Benefits of E-mail Marketing

As mentioned, these e-mail addresses can be used in many different ways, and one of these is through e-mail marketing.

As the name says, e-mail marketing is promoting products and services straight into the inboxes of your target and existing customers.

In the early days when I started talking about using e-mail marketing as one of the methods of earning passive income, most of my mentees would ask: Why would I intrude other people's mailboxes?

Perhaps a much better question is, why should I do e-mail marketing? What is in it for you?

Here are some of the many benefits of e-mail marketing:

It has a wide reach. Remember, almost every person in the Internet has an e-mail address. You may not know where this person lives, but you can reach them and sell your items conveniently when you are able to communicate with them through e-mail.

It is worth the money. Right here right now, I want to get one thing straight: e-mail marketing requires money or investment. Of course, you can go the "free route" by using a free e-mail address, but there are repercussions in doing so, which I will discuss later on.

However, rest assured that e-mail marketing can give you a good return for money. According to Direct Marketing Association, **e-mail marketing provides more than 4,000% return on investment for businesses in the United States.**

It can be automated. One of the best things about e-mail marketing is you do not need to work extensively for it. You see, when you start building your list of subscribers to your e-mail, you will soon realize that you may end up sending e-mails not just to a few dozens but hundreds of people. I know some huge and successful companies already have millions of subscribers! Can you imagine yourself sending an e-mail to each one of them manually? Definitely not!

Thankfully, to help you with e-mail marketing, you can use certain tools such as autoresponders, which I will talk about in a while.

Two Things You Need for E-mail Marketing

When you want to do e-mail marketing, there are two major technical requirements: a landing page and an autoresponder.

What is a landing page? It is basically a webpage that generates the highest attention from your audience. This means it is the page that you design to capture subscribers and ultimately build a list.

What can you see in a typical landing page? The actual content can greatly vary depending on your objective. Normally, they contain the following:

- Introduction, or what the page is about
- Benefits of subscribing to your e-mail list
- Offer, if any (such as an e-book, a product, or any type of freebie)

Passive Income

- Call to action, which features fields where subscribers can add their name and e-mail addresses

To create your call to action button, you would need an mailing list builder or an app that can perform different functions. These include:

- Collect e-mails
- Allow subscribers to add themselves using their mobile devices
- Pop up on the screen once the reader is in the webpage

Aside from the landing page, you are going to need an autoresponder. So what is it? It is a program designed to answer e-mails sent by people such as your subscribers. The application can be very simple or complicated, depending on the features.

But as someone who wants to do e-mail marketing, you definitely need it for a couple of reasons:

- **You want to make sure that your subscribers hear something from you upon signing up.** If you have already signed up for a mailing list, the very first e-mail that you receive is actually from the autoresponder.

    It is incredibly important that your subscriber hears from you as soon as the e-mail address is provided to remove any doubt that you are not real, worse that you are out to scam them. This can be hurtful to your marketing strategies.

- **It saves you time and effort.** As mentioned, autoresponders make e-mailing very easy and convenient. This is because you can send newsletters, e-mails, and other online marketing materials by batches.

- **Track e-mail marketing data.** This matters because you are paying for your autoresponder subscription, and you need to know if you are getting returns from your investments and by how much.

There are several autoresponders available in the market today:

- GetResponse
- AWeber
- MailChimp

Creating Newsletters

What kinds of e-mails do you send? You can actually deliver a plain e-mail to your subscribers, especially if it is just an update or a quick note. However, if you want to make the most out of the strategy, you may want to send a newsletter.

Passive Income

The great thing about newsletters is that information can be condensed in one e-mail and they are visually appealing than plain e-mail. This is important since the goal of doing e-mail marketing is to get subscribers do something, which may be to buy a product, join your community, etc.

How to Earn with E-mail Marketing

By now, you know or at least have the basic idea on how to start your e-mail marketing campaign. At this point, let me tell you why it is a money-making machine for you:

- **Sell stuff.** You can offer a product that may already be available in Amazon or even your e-book. In the previous chapters, I have already shown you how to maximize these two passive income strategies.

- **Do affiliate marketing.** You can use e-mail marketing techniques as part of your affiliate marketing campaign. Introduce the product or service you wish to promote then encourage them to click on the link, buy the product, or subscribe to the service.

    REMEMBER: Use your affiliate link every time you are doing affiliate marketing. Otherwise, all your efforts will be in vain. You will not get any from the sale!

- **Advertise.** This is excellent for people who have already built a good mailing list (or already has several subscribers). You can use this as leverage to approach potential advertisers, or if you are already influential in your industry, they will be the one to seek you out. Depending on the agreement, it is possible to earn more than $10,000 a month from advertising only.

- **Promote your other sources of passive income.** In the succeeding chapters, you will learn at least the basics of creating a viral video or an online course, both of which can be promoted through e-mail marketing.

Important Tips

Before I officially end this chapter, let me leave you with some practical tips to improve your e-mail marketing strategies further:

- **Ensure the privacy of your subscribers.** Include a privacy policy in your landing page and remind them that their information is secured. Do not trade, sell, or exchange their data to anyone. If you want to establish partnerships with other businesses, make sure that you ask permission from your subscribers first before you share their details.

- **Do not request for more personal information.** Limit it to their name and e-mail address—nothing more.

- **Use their name in your e-mails.** What do you think sounds better: Hi, sir, or Hi, Dan? The latter is definitely a much better choice. The more informal the e-mail sounds, the more relatable it feels. It is like sending an e-mail to a friend.

  Autoresponders can be set to send e-mails using the subscriber's name.

- **Perform split testing for your e-mails and landing pages.** Split testing is a process of creating different versions of a single content then checking out which one generates the best results, usually in terms of click-through rate.

  For example, if you are going to split test a landing page, you may have the original content (A) and the alternate version (B), which has a different location of the call to action box. You then publish these two versions and check which one, say, captures the most number of subscribers. You can follow the same model when doing your e-mail marketing.

  Why is split testing important? For two reasons. One, there is no point in spending time and money on a strategy that produces a poorer result. Second, you want to maximize the better option.

- **Schedule e-mail accordingly.** There is nothing that I hate than to be bombarded by several e-mails in a week. Not only does it bury other important e-mails underneath the pile, it is also annoying. Thus, make sure that you schedule your e-mails at appropriate times. It is common to send one newsletter a month and then one long e-mail every two weeks. If you need to send an update, then you can send it right away.

- **Include an unsubscribe button or link.** Definitely, you do not want subscribers to leave, and as a marketer, it is a challenge you need to win. However, giving your subscriber an option is a sign of politeness and respect.

- **Make your offer relevant.** A good way to encourage subscription is to make an offer, which can be an e-book or a report. I have also known of others that offer great discounts on their first purchase once they subscribe to the mailing list. In fact, you can think outside the box, but see to it that your offer makes sense—that is, it relates to what you are really offering or selling.

- **Check that your mail appears good in mobile devices.** Experts say that there will come a time when mobile demand exceeds that of laptops. Truth be told, mobile ecommerce, or shopping using the mobile phone, has been increasing over the last few years. However, it is not only shopping they do—they also check their mails using their mobile devices. For this reason, it is important that your e-mail format is mobile friendly. There are excellent newsletter templates and autoresponders that work well with mobile devices.

- **Offer HTML or text options.** These are the two common general formats of e-mails. Text means that images and videos are not normally seen by the subscribers. While this could be caused by the device's settings and permissions, some people do not want them as they tend to slow down page download.

Chapter 5: Passive Income 4: Affiliate Marketing

* * *

One of the flourishing careers is sales. In fact, I would like to think that if you want to get rich, sales is the skill you need to master. Once you know the tips and tricks of the trade, there is no limit as to what you can sell and, of course, how much income you are going to get.

Usually, when we think of sales, we think of a product. And when we think about the product, we believe that we have to build it from scratch. This can be daunting for some people, especially those who believe they do not have any technical skill or creativity to come up with one.

However, products do not have to necessarily be your own creation. It is possible to sell other people's and that you can do so even when you are online.

This is the general concept of affiliate marketing.

What Is Affiliate Marketing?

As I promised in the previous chapters, I will take the time to talk about affiliate marketing, and we have come to such point.

Affiliate marketing is a marketing strategy that involves the promotion or advertising of other people's products in exchange for a commission, which is normally a percentage of sales.

Basically, your job is like a typical salesperson who works for a company creating products or offering services, although there are a couple of differences:

- **You are an independent contractor.** This simply means that other than the commission you receive, you do not receive other kinds of compensation or benefits from the vendor.

- **There is no training available.** When you are hired by a company, it spends money on your continuing education or training to ensure that you will always have the most updated knowledge and expertise in selling. There is nothing like it when you are doing affiliate marketing, although, in some cases, vendors may provide tools and resources to help you out.

- **No person is going to pressure you to sell something.** When you are working for a company as a salesperson, you can expect your manager to be breathing down your neck when you are only breaking even or not hitting your quota. After all, sales is your job, and you need to do it right. This also implies that unlike in affiliate marketing, having a regular sales job means you can also get fired.

Benefits of Affiliate Marketing

A lot of people I know who are earning passive income are affiliate marketers. If you are wondering why it is such a popular form of earning money on the side, let me outline its top benefits:

- **Unlimited Income Opportunities.** As I mentioned many times before, one of the best things about earning passive income is there is no limited when it comes to your earning potential. It is the same thing with affiliate marketing.

    You may say, "But you are only earning a commission!" That is true, and to put everything in a proper perspective, your commission, which is usually percentage of sales, is not very high. In fact, it is incredibly rare to find vendors that offer 10% of the purchase price as your commission. It can be as low as a percent!

But why would you still do it? Let us do the math. A product worth $50 has a 3% commission. Each month, you can sell 100 of these. Therefore, every 30 days, you can earn $150 or $1,800 annually.

However, this is just one product! What if you have three more that is worth the same price and with the same number of sales each month?

- **Passion.** Here is another beautiful reason to do affiliate marketing. You see, when you are a traditional marketer, it is possible to be asked to sell a product that you do not really want or do not have excellent knowledge about. That can be a problem since you may come across as less convincing compared to when you are offering a product that you are very familiar with.

  With so many products and services you can choose from under an affiliate program, there is no doubt in my mind you can find at least five that is up to your liking. This makes affiliate marketing even more fun for you.

- **Less Stress.** This is because you are not creating the product yourself. All you need to do is to promote it—that is it. The lack of product to sell means you do not have to maintain any inventory, which requires space or investments on technology like an inventory management software. You do not even have to do any fulfillment or accounting. Just wait for the commission to be credited into your account.

How to Become an Affiliate Marketer

In this section, I wish to show you the different pathways you can take so you can officially start earning your affiliate marketing commission:

Amazon Associates

There are a number of reasons why I am predisposed to this affiliate program:

- Amazon is one of the leading and the biggest marketplaces in the world. This means you have thousands of products to choose from, including their own.
- Their affiliate program has been around for a long time, which suggests it is well designed and trustworthy.
- Many customers are familiar, trust, and use Amazon.
- Amazon has an excellent fulfillment program, which, in case you forgot, can also help you earn a passive income.

James Cheney

- The affiliate program already includes helpful tools such as those that can help you make reports so you can track your income properly.
- You have the potential to earn 10% advertising fee, although the actual percentage depends on the product and the volume of your sales. For instance, the fixed advertising fee rate for electronic products is 4%. For general products, you can earn 4% for a sales volume of 1 to 6. You can refer to the two boxes below for guidance (list as of 2016).

Product Category	Fixed Advertising Fee Rates
Electronics Products	4.00%
Television Products	2.00%
PC Component Products	2.50%
Kindle tablets, Kindle e-readers, and Fire Phone	4.00%
Amazon Fire TV and Echo	7.00%
Amazon MP3 Products	5.00%
Amazon Video Products	5.00%
Game Downloads Products	10.00%
Gift Cards Redeemable on amazon.com	6.00%
Gift Cards Not Redeemable on amazon.com	4.00%
Amazon Coins	10.00%
Grocery Products (including Prime Pantry)	4.00%
Video Game Console Products	1.00%
Headphones Products	6.00%
DVD Products	4.00%
Industrial Products	8.00%
Handmade Products	4.00%

Passive Income

Number of Products Shipped/Downloaded in a Given Month**	Volume-Based Advertising Fee Rates for General Products
1-6	4.00%
7-30	6.00%
31-110	6.50%
111-320	7.00%
321-630	7.50%
631-1570	8.00%
1571-3130	8.25%
3131+	8.50%

Independent Websites

Do you have a product or service that you will be more than happy to promote for a commission? You can follow these easy steps:

- Go to Google or any of your preferred search engines.
- Type (name of the product, could be general) and "affiliate program." So if you wish to sell pet carriers, you therefore search "pet carriers affiliate program."
- The search results will then show you the websites or vendors that offer such affiliate programs.

- Select the most ideal for you.

Another option is to simply visit an e-commerce website that you normally check out or even buy stuff from then scroll all the way down, where you can see some more links. Find the link that says "Affiliate," "Affiliate Program," "Associate," or "Associate Program."

Affiliate Marketplaces

The above-mentioned method works, but it can be frustrating sometimes, especially if the websites or vendors do not have an affiliate program, you are not qualified to participate, or you are not happy with the advertising fees.

If you want the most number of options, I strongly suggest that you go to Affiliate Marketplaces. This works similarly like Amazon, where you can find a treasure trove of products and services to sell, but the biggest difference is these are listed by vendors who are looking for affiliate marketers. In other words, these are guaranteed to be affiliate programs.

As a marketplace, you can search for affiliate programs based on the products they offer, commission, and even reviews from other affiliate marketers. You can also connect with other marketers, which can be extremely helpful when you are starting out. Many of them will be happy to get you on track.

Some of the most popular affiliate marketplaces are:

- Clicksure
- Clickbank
- CJ
- Payzeno

Joint Venture or Partnership

This strategy can be useful if you still want an independent vendor, but it does not have an affiliate program. Send them a correspondence, informing them of your intention to sell their product for a commission that both of you can agree upon. Normally, businesses do not want to miss the chance of having extra help in marketing, but the problem comes in when it comes to how much they are willing to pay for you. This simply means that you need to level your expectations.

A good way to reduce the rejection is to come up with a range of percentage of sales. You can base your range on what its competitors are offering, the products they are selling, your skills in marketing, and the financial position of the company.

NOTE: Do not expect to get a response right away. In fact, be ready to be rejected a lot of times. However, if you think this is worth it, then by all means pursue it, although I would suggest that you build your credibility and skill as an affiliate marketer first by doing the other methods I mentioned a while ago.

More Tips in Affiliate Marketing

1. **Consider the following when you are looking for a good affiliate program or marketplace:**

   - Products they are selling
   - Reputation of the vendor or the marketplace
   - Average earnings per sale
   - Commission or advertising fee
   - Technical and customer support
   - Marketing materials, which may include banner ads and links
   - Frequency of new product releases
   - Method and frequency of payouts
   - Reviews from other affiliate marketers
   - Requirements to become an affiliate
   - Market trends (Is the product you are trying to promote already has a market? Is that your preferred market?)
   - Competition
   - Conversion rates of the product

2. Limit your affiliate products. Do not be greedy! Otherwise, you will have a hard time marketing each one of the products.

When you are starting, choose one product to promote, but make sure it is something you can be deeply involved in. If you already have an online business or product or service, then find an affiliate product that is relevant to it.

For example, if you are in the business of selling online courses, you may look for affiliate programs for practical exams or other online courses that you are not planning to offer.

As you build your skill in affiliate marketing, you can then proceed to adding two or three more. As for me, I prefer to deal with at most five high-quality products with excellent conversion rates, market, credibility, and payout process.

Further, to maximize my affiliate programs, I select related ones. I am currently promoting pet carriers (that is why I talk about it so much), but I also signed up for affiliate programs for pet supplies, pet food, and even pet travel. This way, when I promote one, I can also market the others with ease.

3. Promote your products in different ways. Here are some of the well-known strategies in promoting your affiliate products:

- Blog
- E-mail marketing
- E-books and courses
- Infographic
- Reviews
- Social media
- Forums and communities
- Websites
- Search engine optimization (SEO)
- Search engine marketing like Google AdWords

Of all these, I prefer using a blog, e-mail marketing, and reviews for one good reason: information.

It is human instinct to be curious, ask questions, and assess products and services before you pay for them. And a good way to help your customers make better decisions, increase your credibility in the industry, build trust and relationship with your target market, and eventually make them loyal customers is to teach them. Give them the right information and tools to decide, make the most of their money, and find products that they truly need.

Although the marketing techniques I shared can do that, the BIG THREE, as I call them, have provided me the biggest return on investment.

VERY IMPORTANT: I have decided to make this the last point not because it is the least important but it is the most essential thing to remember when it comes to affiliate marketing: be patient.

Nobody wants to be pressured to buy something, more so from someone they do not know like you. Thus, you need to build your credibility and reputation first to win the trust of your target market, and this process takes time. The good thing is as long as you maintain your positive reputation, your efforts will pay off handsomely.

Chapter 6 : Passive Income 5: Create an Online Course

* * *

One of my greatest childhood dreams was to be a teacher. I was greatly inspired by an elementary teacher of mine. For some reason, however, I was not able to pursue it, but that is beside the point.

What I want to point out is this: The reason why I want to teach is because I want to impart knowledge and information to anyone. It is also my motivation why I came up with this e-book.

And it looks like I am not the only one who has such desire. More people are becoming generous of their expertise, helping others to succeed, by creating online courses.

What Is an Online Course?

Traditional classes work this way: You select a school, a program, or a course. Sign up, pay your tuition fee, and make sure that you can attend your classes. In between the enrollment and the end of the program are dozens of exams, quizzes, and what have you that you need to pass in order to meet the objectives of the program, which may be to receive a certificate or a diploma, move on to the next level, or receive credits.

Online courses work that way with a very significant difference: you take these classes on the Internet.

In online courses, you select a school, a program, or a course. You sign up then pay your tuition fee. However, many of them have a more flexible schedule, so you have the opportunity to complete the program at your own pace and time. Sometimes the course has its duration, which may be a few weeks or months, but as long as you can meet the requirements and complete the course before time is up, you are still eligible for a certification, diploma, or other incentives.

Why do many people like online courses?

- **They can be cheap.** Many online courses are not free, but usually they are far cheaper than when they are compared with traditional courses. And even if the costs are comparable, students can enjoy savings in transport, food, and accommodation.

- **They offer flexibility.** Coursera, one of the biggest websites to offer several online courses, allow members to enroll in certain programs and complete them in stages. This relieves the pressure on users who may have a full-time job and may, at some point, lack the time to complete the entire course at the required time.

While you can enroll in online courses, you can also make money out of them. Yes, you can generate passive income by creating your own.

Benefits of Creating an Online Course

Anyone who is thinking of earning passive income should seriously consider making online courses for the following reasons:

They are profitable and lucrative. The online course industry was already worth $57 billion in 2014, according to Forbes. The business magazine further predicted that it could increase to $100 billion. We still have to verify that, but the bottom line is the demand is increasing, and people are willing to pay for these types of programs.

Moreover, to give you an idea on how profitable it can be, imagine this: You create a short course worth $20. Very cheap, right? But then, you also have 50 students. This means that in one course alone, you can earn $1,000!

However, most programs do not end in one course, and it is not uncommon for subscribers to demand for more comprehensive courses later, especially if they appreciate and see the value of your courses. So you can add as many courses as you like and double and triple your income.

Not only that, there are other ways on how to make more money from the online courses, which I will show you later.

They can be very easy to make. One of the reasons why some people are apprehensive about creating courses is they think they could not do it. "I am not an expert!" or "I do not think I am credible enough to teach or make these courses." These statements may be true, but usually, they are not entirely correct. Every person has the ability to make excellent courses, and you will know why later.

How to Design an Online Course

Creating an online course will be challenging in the beginning, but once you get the hang of it, and you can replicate the system, you will be amazed on how many courses you can come up with and, most importantly, sell to your target market.

But before we get into marketing your online courses, you need to come up with one first. Let us begin.

Topic

Of course, the very first thing to consider when you want to make a course is your topic. What will be the course about?

Go deep into your knowledge. What is it that you are good at? Are you great at gardening? Do you know how to code? Or perhaps you have a talent in sleeping faster? Sometimes the ideas that you have may sound silly, but let me tell you, these days, there is a market for almost everything!

> But I suggest you write everything you think you are good at down in a sheet of paper to make sure that you do not forget about them.

Market

Now that you have a pretty good idea of the things that you can teach or share, it is time to determine the people who will BENEFIT THE MOST from the learning. To do this, you need to be more specific of your knowledge. For example, what exactly about gardening are you good at? Is it urban gardening? Then there is a good chance that your target market are city dwellers or people who live in small homes or tight spaces.

It is also important that you pay more attention to the industry, especially the trends. I know of many online course designers who are able to sell their very new and novel products, but for starters, it is best to stick with the ones that you are more likely to have an existing or growing market.

Format of the Course

You already have the topic and the market. At this point, you are ready to create your online course. But which format should it be? There are so many options to choose from:

***Downloads*–** These are courses that can be downloaded in the mobile devices or laptops of your subscribers. They can be in the form of PDF, word processor (like Word), audio file, or a video.

These files are stored in a secure server or a cloud host such as Dropbox, and a link is delivered to their e-mail, so they can choose where they want to save the file.

The great thing about this is that learning can continue or proceed even if the user is already offline or no longer connected to the Internet. This is the reason why it is extremely popular for both course creators and their subscribers.

TIPS:

- Consider compressing the file if it is already big. Otherwise, the subscriber will have a hard time downloading it.
- You can also break down large files into small parts (part 1, part 2, etc.).
- After they have signed up for the course, make sure you remind the subscriber to check their e-mail for the link. If they cannot find the link in their inbox, remind them to check their Spam or Junk Mail

folder, as well as to add your e-mail address in the white list.
- Label your downloadable files properly.

Membership – You can also hit two birds in one stone: build your subscribers and offer an online course. You can do that by creating a membership website. In this setup, subscribers are provided with either a link of the membership site, which is not available or seen by non-subscribers, or login details, the password of which may be changed by the subscribers later.

Inside the membership site, subscribers can now download, watch, read, or listen to the online courses, as well as network with other subscribers. Coursera is a good example of a membership site, although the membership is free.

TIP: If you are planning this strategy for promoting and selling online courses, you see to it that you are offering PREMIUM to your subscribers. Provide them with exclusive features, resources, tools, or courses which means these are not available to non-subscribers.

Live – You can also provide online courses live, which means you have the chance to interact with your subscribers. Your "students" will be able to ask questions, leave feedback, or answer your questions. Some people like this setup since they are able to get to know you properly, and it adds the element of fun and dynamics to online courses.

TIPS:

- Make sure that you have a stable connection. Inform your subscribers in different intervals as to the schedule of the live discussion. Usually, you send an e-mail once they have signed up. Then you make a follow-up three days after, a day before the course, and a few hours before it. Of course, the actual interval depends on the timeline for the courses.

- Use slides, videos, or screencasts during the course discussion. You can also share your screen to your subscribers.

- Provide them a downloadable copy of the course, so they can review it at any time.

Websites for Courses – Lastly, you can make a course then sell it in websites such as Udemy, Stacksocial, Coursera, Lynda, and Udacity. Just remember, however, that they may have preferences as to the type of courses they wish to accept. For example, Coursera courses are mostly in partnership with universities and colleges in the United States, with real professors conducting the trainings. Lynda, on the other hand, is more focused on business-oriented or related courses.

How to Market Online Courses

Passive Income

Here are some of the effective ways to market your online courses:

- Blog
- Social media
- E-mail marketing
- Websites
- Reviews
- Partnerships with other course creators

But one of the most effective strategies is **offering a free course**. You have read it right. When you offer a free course, you can:

- Give your subscribers an idea of how the succeeding courses are going to be like.
- Make them understand the benefit they are going to enjoy if they continue with the courses.
- Provide them an overview.
- Show off your expertise and skills.

Your free course does not have to be long, but it should be specific or professional enough to convince your subscribers that you are a subject matter expert, and they are going to receive valuable information from your courses.

Pricing

How much should you charge per course? The best way to gauge is to know how much your competitors are pricing their courses. Then you can go a little bit higher or lower than that, depending on the actual course design, target audience, length of the course, and other incentives given upon signing up.

Experts, however, suggest not to go too low with your course price for a number of reasons:

- Usually, cheap equals poor quality. You do not want to give them that signal.
- You want to work with high-quality subscribers. These are people who are definitely serious in learning and are more than likely to order other courses from you.

When it comes to pricing structure, you can:

- Charge the entire course
- Consider installments especially if the course is already $300 and above
- Offer discounts upon signing up
- Offer discounts to those with referrals
- Increase costs in each course level
- Charge for subscription of the membership website or access to several courses

Chapter 7: Passive Income 6: Create Viral Videos

* * *

Do you know Justin Bieber? Perhaps you have heard his songs played over and over on the radio, or you have at least come across his name in entertainment news. He is such a big star for such a young age. He is barely 23, but he already has a net worth of $200 million!

While he is such a huge phenomenal star, some people do not know how he ended up in the entertainment industry. It all started in YouTube, where he started posting videos of him singing. Usher, another well-known R&B sensation, heard him, and as they say, the rest is history.

He, however, is just one of the growing number of music artists that started their careers in the world's biggest video channel called YouTube. Boyce Avenue has already toured several countries, but the group began by covering mainstream songs. The late Christina Grimmie, who was one of the top finalists in *The Voice*, also began by making covers and posting them in YouTube.

And it is not only singers who are making waves in the websites. PewDiePie has a net worth of $12 million as of

2015, and he has made a name by making reviews of different computer games.

Surely you are wondering, "How did they do that?" How are they able to earn such income or open opportunities for themselves just by posting videos? The answer is because they have created videos that have already become viral.

What Is a Viral Video?

Psy, a Korean artist, was basically unheard of until he uploaded his music video for his song "Gangnam Style." It was so popular that YouTube had to adjust its viewing counter. Eventually, it is one of the videos that earned a BILLION views.

The video, however, would not have achieved such status if it did not go viral. As its name suggests, viral means the file—which can be an image, video, audio, or even a document—has been shared over and over for a very short amount of time.

In other words, to be considered viral, a video must meet two requirements: (1) it has been shared several times across different platforms especially social media and (2) the spread of the file should occur within a very short amount of time. Psy's second viral video for "Gentleman" was viewed 38 million times within 24 hours since its upload!

Passive Income

How Do You Make Money in a Viral Video?

Before I tell you the different tips and tricks to make your video viral, let us discuss first what is in it for you if your video becomes viral. Why does it matter anyway? To answer the question, let us talk about monetization.

There are many different ways to achieve that:

- **Participate in YouTube and Google's monetization program.** When you enable monetization of your videos through this program, you allow Google and YouTube, as well as their industry partners, to advertise in your YouTube video through Adsense ads or a full commercial. This is basically the one that appears before the actual video plays (yes, it is the one that you can skip).

- **Partner with advertisers.** Many YouTube influencers, or those that have already established a huge following, are often sought out by advertisers themselves for a variety of reasons. It could be they want these creators to feature their products or make a review. It is also not impossible for creators to produce videos for these companies. In exchange, they earn a fee, which can be substantial.

- **Build a brand.** Videos can also be used to build a brand and establish a bigger, closer community of subscribers and followers. These are the people who are more likely to take advantage of what you are promoting, whether it is a product or a service. You can also use your videos to showcase the features and benefits of your business or product, further adding to their credibility.

Always remember: it is easier for you to market products and services to people who trust you, but for you to gain their trust, you need to prove that you are deserving of it.

- **Merchandise and affiliates.** This is partly related to the previous point, although this is more specific. Usually, many YouTube stars venture into creating souvenirs or merchandise to further improve and maximize their branding and engagement with their subscribers.

How to Make Your Video Viral

Are the reasons making you excited to make your first video and make it viral? Then good! You are ready to know what it takes to do it:

Video Subject

The very first thing to consider is your video subject. What is it going to be? Many video creators have a niche, and it is usually what they are good at. For example, if you love to do DIY, then show off how you have hacked an Ikea furniture. Do you think you are funny? Then by all means share your comedy.

When it comes to making videos for monetization, you are free to think outside the box provided that the video you have created does not go against the terms and conditions.

TIPS:

1. The more unique the video, the more likely they will go viral. Go find "Will It Blend" channel in YouTube.
2. Make a storyboard or create a script so you can come up with a more polished cohesive video.
3. Pay attention to the length of the video. You have to think about your audience. Do they have time to sit and watch a video for 15 minutes? If not, perhaps it is better to break your videos into parts or series, which you can upload at different times so you can encourage your subscribers to keep coming back.

Production

Once you already have a vision or idea of what and how your video is going to be, you can proceed to production. Again, there are no hard and fast rules in creating viral videos. If you can check out Vines or videos shared in Twitter, they are commonly shot by a camera phone. We have also seen many videos, normally personal entries, recorded using a regular webcam.

However, if you are dead serious in making money in viral videos, then you need to invest, especially in equipment. For instance, if you are a travel video blog, it makes perfect sense to get yourself a Go Pro or even a drone for a more cinematic effect of the video. You may also want to pay for:

- Excellent lighting
- Props
- Special effects and video editing software
- Audio equipment like microphones and recorders
- A more professional video camera

Shooting and Editing

Is your equipment prepared? Then you are ready to shoot. The location, people involved, scenarios, props etc., are all based on the idea or concept you wish to achieve. This is why a storyboard or a script is handy: you will know what you will need during the actual shoot.

The shoot itself is not so much of a problem—editing is. A poorly edited video can easily lose its effect on the audience and can convey the wrong message about the brand you are trying to build.

Never, ever skip editing a video, and make sure that you do not upload any raw file to avoid accidentally sharing it to your subscribers. Nevertheless, edit accordingly—that is, do not go overboard that the video itself can already look fake.

Publishing

The video is ready! Where do you share it? Of course, the easiest and quickest answer is YouTube, and I highly recommend that you make this a priority. However, this is not the only place where you can upload the video. You can also share it at:

- Facebook
- Twitter
- Instagram
- Vimeo
- Reddit
- Forums or message boards
- Blog
- Website

You can share the video directly or add a link.

TIP: Choose a central location for the video. This means that even if you share it at different places, they all should point to one place. In this case, you can upload the video in YouTube and use the sharing button. You can also embed the video code into your website or blog, as well as forums or message boards. If you are using other video channels, do not forget to add your YouTube channel in your bio.

Tracking

The video is uploaded. Your next job is to track its views. This is not much of a problem because social media sites such as Facebook already has counters, and Google or YouTube provides you with the analytics tools and statistics report.

What should be more important is the classification of the views. If you are trying to monetize your video, particularly in Google, you should aim for constantly increasing your unique views.

Other Tips in Creating Viral Videos

- As YouTube likes to emphasize, quality videos first over money.
- Make your YouTube posting more regular. You do not need to post videos every single day, but at least establish a pattern so your subscribers can already anticipate when to visit your page.
- Encourage subscription! Do not be afraid to run promos to increase subscription and viewership.
- Be patient. In many cases, you will not get it the first time. The most important thing is each time, you get to increase your subscription and viewership.

Chapter 8: Passive Income 7: Trading Domain Names

* * *

I often like to compare cyberspace with the real world because the truth is the Internet is more or less a reflection of what we have right here, right now, offline.

For example, I usually refer to the e-mail address as your residential address in the Internet. It's how people find you and leave you communication, among other things. It's also how you can get access to more benefits offered by the myriad of websites online.

There's also the domain name, which I prefer to liken to a street. It points out to the exact address or location of your IP address. I'll try to explain these terms more comprehensively in a while.

But know that domain names are what separate one website from the other, and if you're interested in generating passive income online, they can also provide good revenue by learning how to trade them.

James Cheney

Understanding Domain Names

For the non-techie readers, let me explain domain names first before I proceed to the to-dos when you like to trade domain names.

Domain names are often confused by other terms such as uniform resource location (URL) and even an e-mail address.

Domain names are basically a specific unique address that points out to a specific unique IP address. Does it sound more confusing? Let's put it this way.

Every computer, server, or network is provided with its own IP (Internet protocol) address. The computer you're using that is connected online has one. While an IP address can be changed, it cannot be shared with anyone else. This address is composed of a series of numbers, which a lot of people cannot memorize. So to make it much easier to remember, we now have a domain name, which is its text version.

A URL, on the other hand, refers to the complete address of the webpage, which is designated by http:// as in http://www.coolstory.com.

A domain name is composed of different parts offered to as labels. Two general classifications are top level and second level. The top-level domains are the ones you may be familiar with. These include .com (commercial), .info (information), .biz (business), and .edu (education). For those who are running or maintaining a government website, the top-level domain is often .gov.

The second-level domain is what comes AFTER the top-level domain. It is often an abbreviation of a geographical location or a generic term such as *.fashion*, *.marketing*, or *.estate*. For example, if it says coolstory.com.us, *us* is the second-level domain while *.com* is the top-level domain. How about www.? This one is actually referred as the subdomain.

Also know that a domain name is different from a website, which is already a collection of different webpages, each of which has its own URL. You need to have a domain name to have a website, but it's possible to not have a website while you own a domain name.

The Power of Trading Domain Names

When we say trading domain names, we mean buying and selling of domain names (or it can just be selling) for the purpose of generating a profit. Many people are already engaged in this simply because it can be lucrative. When the domain name business.com was sold in 1999, it fetched a cool $350 million!

The likelihood of earning this much in a single domain is few and far between, but still, if you know how to trade, your returns are much higher than the investment.

How to Trade a Domain Name

There are two types of domain names that you can trade: used and non-used.

1. Have a good idea of what domain name will probably sell. The hottest domain names are those that are generic such as drugs.com, newspaper.com, books.com, etc. Not only are they very common words, they are much easier to remember.

However, their advantage can also be their disadvantage. Because they are already common, there's a good chance that they are already used or are also traded. If they are traded, you have a couple of options:

- What types of top-level domain names have been registered? If the .com is already registered, then try to check out if .biz, .info, and other top-level domain names have also been registered.

- Are they registered to a specific second-level domain? This works if your target buyers are located in a specific region or niche.

- Do you have the money to buy the domain? To know, you need to contact the domain name's owner.

But how do you exactly do that? You can perform a whois search. Enter the domain name, press Lookup, and the system will generate a list of information about the domain name, including the name of the registrant, address, and e-mail address.

Note, though, that as a way of protecting their privacy, especially against spamming, several domain name owners will use a service that conceals contact information.

If you can't do any of the above, then the next best thing is to create an entirely new domain name. In creating your own domain name, remember to keep it simple. As much as possible, avoid hyphens and misspellings.

WARNING: Do not try to register a domain name bearing a trademark (e.g., Adidas.com). This is a form of cybersquatting and is punishable by law.

2. Register your domain name.

Once you already have a domain name in mind, it's time to register it. You have a lot of choices for this, but one of the best is Godaddy. For illustration, we're also going to use the website:

- Enter the domain name you like. Press Search Domain.
- Check out the available domain names. Can you find it on the list? If it is not there, it means it's already been taken.
- Begin searching for a new domain or choose among the list. Press Select. (You can select as many domain names as you want.)
- Press Continue to Cart if you're ready to pay.
- View the other add-ons. Add the things you want to add, but since our purpose is to just register a domain name, you can skip them.
- Pay for the domain name registration, which is usually through a credit card.

That's it! Your domain name is already registered and it's up for trading.

Now what if you are already using your domain name and you want to trade or sell it for a profit? You can use valuation tools such as Estibot and Valuate. These websites use different metrics or algorithms to come up with an estimate. Again, since it's an estimate, the actual trading price can be lower or higher, but at least you have a pretty good solid idea.

Keep in mind that you have the option to sell domain along with the entire website. If the buyer doesn't want your content, however, you may lose it forever unless you secure it in case you're planning to get a new domain name.

Passive Income

Important Tips in Trading Domain Names

- Domain name registration is pretty cheap, so you can register as many as you like. I recommend you do this too to make sure that your competitors won't have a similar-sounding domain name.
- However, remember that domain name registration ends and it has to be renewed every year. Therefore, you have to consider the cost of maintaining these domains.
- Allow others to see your contact information. If you're scared of being spammed, create an entirely different e-mail for domain name registration.
- Promote your available domain name! Use the marketing techniques I shared in the previous chapters.

Conclusion

* * *

I always believe that if a person wants to achieve a complete financial freedom, he or she needs to know how to earn passive income. It can provide you with the time you need to pursue other interests and achieve a much better work-life balance.

Before I officially end the e-book, I'd like to leave you with my food for thought and key takeaways:

- There are many, many ways to earn passive income online—some are more complicated or difficult than the others, some offering higher income than the rest. The most important thing is you have choices. You can pursue one that fits your needs, preferences, knowledge or expertise, training potential, and a whole lot of other factors.

- Earning passive income doesn't mean you don't have to do anything anymore. First of all, income doesn't happen suddenly. It takes weeks or months before it builds up to a good level.

    Further, even if you've already found considerable success in your passive income strategy, you still need to time and money to constantly improve your technique, product and marketing.

- However, once you beat the learning curve, everything comes easy. There are also many ways on how to automate several processes in generating passive income. For example, you can use inventory management software if you want to do an Amazon FBA or utilize an auto responder for e-mail marketing. Once you've set the foundation, you can choose to update only certain parts, so you spend less time and money than before.

- You can replicate the passive income system — this is one of the best things about online strategies I have shared. Of course, the systems for marketing product A and product B are not 100 percent the same — they can differ in terms of target market or cost — but the processes can be very similar, which means you don't need to go through baby steps all the time.

- You can diversify your passive income. In fact, I highly recommend it. You may diversify in terms of the products you offer in affiliate marketing or choose one or two — or all of the methods I shared in this book.

I hope that I have shared something valuable to you and that you will go on to take action and create your own passive streams of income.

James Cheney

Finally, if you enjoyed this book, then I'd like to ask you for a favor, would you be
kind enough to leave a review for this book on Amazon? It'd be greatly
appreciated!

www.ingramcontent.com/pod-product-compliance
Lightning Source LLC
Chambersburg PA
CBHW060412190526
45169CB00002B/869